OUR TOWN

A Guide For Studying Any Community

Written by **Dianne Draze**
Illustrated by **Dean** and **Pat Crawford**

Edited by **Sonsie Conroy**

ISBN 0-931724-48-1

Contents

For the Instructor

What Do You Know?

Were your community's founders gold miners or farmers? Does your town's name mean "mud hole" or "beautiful view?" Is "downtown" maturing, dying, or being reborn? Can you boast about being a busy harbor, a historic site, or a recreational wonderland? Is your community more like a raging river or a quiet pond? If you (or your students) don't know all the many fascinating things about the place you call home, it's time to find out.

About Our Town

Here's *Our Town*, a guide for studying a community. Whether you and your students live in a city, town, suburb, hamlet, village, or burgh, you can use the ideas in this text to learn about your surroundings.

Since *Our Town* is designed to be used with primary students, the main emphasis of the unit is to make students aware of the many aspects that combine to make their community a unique one. As a result of taking part in the activities in *Our Town*, they should come away with an increased awareness of their community as well as a generalized understanding of the many aspects of community life

Our Town includes a variety of educational experiences. There are ideas for group lessons, group projects, individual projects, learning centers, and worksheets. All activities are open-ended so they can be used equally well in a large city or in a small town. Use of any of these should be dictated by the needs of your students and the unique character of your community. Some instructors may wish to add their own lessons or discussion sessions in order to emphasize important information about their community.

This is not a unit that uses a textbook and keeps students tied to their classroom. Plan on getting out of the classroom and taking numerous field trips in your community. Arrange to have parents and volunteers share their expertise. Collect any and all information you can about your community—pictures (old and new), relics from the past, maps, business cards and advertisements, brochures, guides, bus schedules, listings of recreational and cultural events, and newspapers. Make this a hands-on unit. Get students involved in asking questions, walking, looking, listening, surveying, categorizing, touching, making, doing, and, most importantly, thinking.

Concepts

Because this unit will be different each time it is taught, depending on the community being studied and the resources that are available, specific behavioral objectives have not been provided. Instead, several generalized concepts that can apply to almost any community are listed below. In addition to these, instructors may wish to add other concepts that are particular to their area.

General Knowledge

- Many things combine to make a community what it is—people, places, businesses, geography, services, attractions, natural resources, and location.

- Our community offers a variety of businesses, services, and opportunites for recreation and education, as well as places to live.
- Communities (cities, towns, villages) are unique and special.
- There are good and bad things about each community.

Location

- Communities have geographical locations. They can be located on a map in relation to other geographical references.
- The location of most communities was originally chosen because of the advantages offered by the geographical location (natural resources, access to water, transportation links).
- Each location has advantages and disadvantages.

History

- The history of a community includes the people who settled there, the reasons why they came to the location, and the events that followed.
- All communities change over time; some faster and to a greater extent than others.
- Communities usually have celebrations to commemorate special events in their history.
- It is important to preserve the history of the community as well as plan for the future.
- History is happening now. It is all around you.

People

- Communities exist to efficiently satisfy the needs (social, economic, cultural, and recreational) of people.
- Communities are made of people who depend on one another.
- Living together in a community allows for division of labor, collective use of services (like police and fire protection), and other advantages such as cultural exposure and availability of products and services.
- All communities need good citizens.

Transportation

- Transportation includes highways and streets for automobiles, buses, bicycles, and trucks, walkways for pedestrians, subways, airports, railroads, monorails, and shipping ports.

Economy

- People work at many different jobs, offering services or producing and selling products.
- A community is made of many different kinds of businesses.

Buildings and Housing

- Communities are places for people to live as well as to work and satisfy needs.
- Buildings are often grouped according to use.
- Styles of buildings and homes reflect the climate, terrain, available building materials, and sometimes the cultural heritage of the area.

Communication

- Information is shared through several forms of communication, including newspaper, telephone, radio, and television.
- Communication networks link the people in a community with each other and with other places.

Education and Recreation

- There are several forms of recreation found in communities. These include parks, athletics, theaters (movies, drama, dance, music), and zoos.
- Most communities have museums that provide people with opportunities for education.
- Schools are an important element of a community.
- Celebrations provide opportunities for recreation and getting together with other people in the community.

Government

- All communities have some form of government with rules and laws.
- The government keeps order in the town, makes and enforces laws, collects taxes, and provides various services.
- Some of the services provided by governments are police and fire protection, hospitals and mental health, garbage and sewer, water, schools, parks and recreation, transportation and streets, planning, and libraries.

Group Projects, Learning Centers, and Lessons

Group Projects

These projects must be done with several people. It will work best if the instructor organizes and oversees these projects. Instructors do not have to do all of these activites. Choose only the projects that best meet the needs and abilities of students and make use of your available resources.

Our Community Quilt

Make a quilt of your community. Have each person make a square that shows something special about your community. Sew the squares together to make a quilt. Hang it where other people can see it.

Our Town Display

Make a display for the entire school that shows something about your community. Some ideas might be:

- historical relics
- pictures showing styles of buildings
- a map showing points of interest or historical significance
- a photographic display of the many things that make a community.

Tour Guide

Make a tourists' guide to your community. As a group, make a list of everything there is to see and do in your community. Give each student a place of interest. Have each student write a page of the booklet about his or her place, giving addresses, hours of operation, brief description and any historical information. Duplicate booklets and give to each person in the class to share with out-of-town visitors.

3-D Model

Make a three-dimensional map of the central part of your community. Assign each person a building or section of the community. Buildings need not be done with great detail, but relative size is important. Use cardboard, boxes, or styrofoam. Color code building to show uses (sell goods, offer services, are governmental agencies, or something else).

Mural

Make a mural showing all the things that go on in your community on a typical day. First, as a group, make a list of typical activities. Try to include a variety of activities. Then mark off a large piece of paper in sections to accomodate the various activities. Assign students to illustrate an activity in a given area of the mural.

Photographic Display

As a group, talk about all the things that make a community or city (people, places to live, places to work, recreation, government, etc.). Discuss what you would like other people to know about your community. Then have each student take pictures of your community. Put the pictures together into a photographic display or slide show that shows what is special about your community. If you choose to do a slide presentation, write dialogue to accompany the slides and tape record the dialogue.

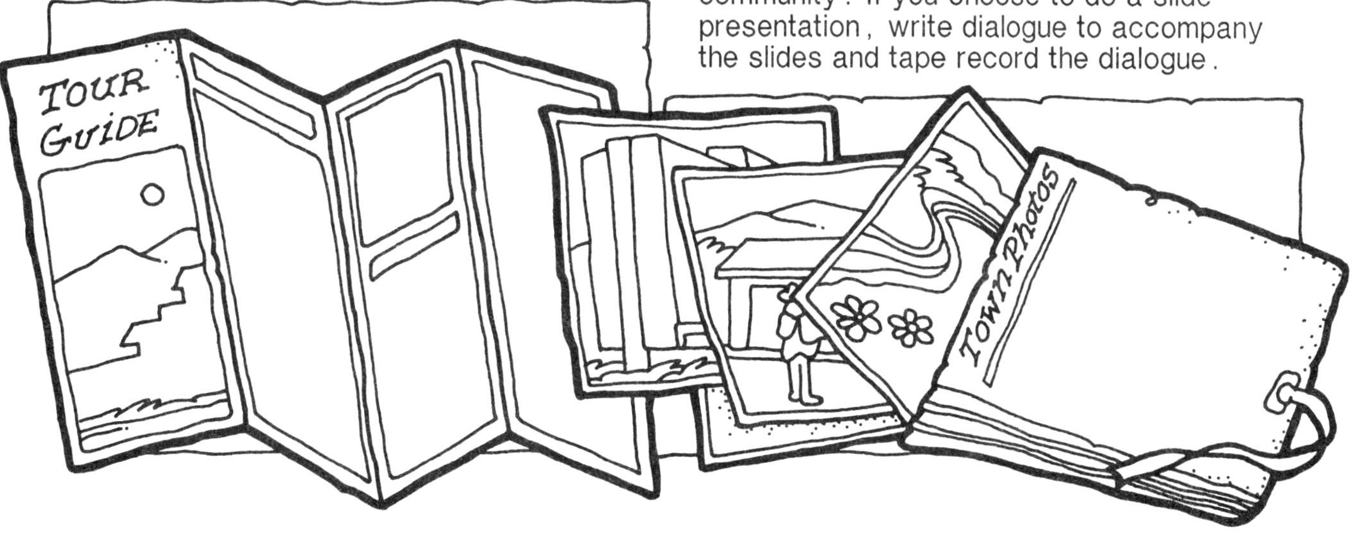

Cityscape

On a large piece of mural paper, make an outline of the skyline of a city. Assign each person a section of the skyline with the instructions to draw a building or business you would find in a city or community. When the group drawing is complete, discuss any one of the following:

- Are uses compatible?
- What else does a city need?
- Are there duplicate uses?

Shopping Center

Do the same project as above, only with a shopping center. Make a large drawing or map of a shopping center. Assign each person a space and have him/her draw a business for that space. Upon completion, discuss:

- Why do we build shopping centers?
- What kind of businesses are usually found in shopping centers?
- What are the advantages and disadvantages of shopping centers?
- If you were a merchant in the downtown community area, how would you feel about a shopping center?
- Why didn't we have shopping centers 100 years ago?

Community Project

Find something in your community that needs to be done and do it. Look for people who need help or companionship, a place that needs to be cleaned up, something (a tree, park, historic building) that needs to be saved, improved, or made safer. Let students choose the project they would like to undertake that will make their community a better place to live.

Time Line

Make a large time line and display in a prominent place in the room. As you learn about different happenings in your community's history, mark these things on the time line. Along with things that are important to the city in general, mark things like when the school was built, when the students entered kindergarten, when they will graduate from high school, etc.

Weekend Scavenger Hunt

Have a weekend scavenger hunt. Send students home on Friday with a list of things they are to search for over the weekend. Select items that are relevant to your community. Some ideas might be:

- The name of someone who has lived in our community over 30 years.
- The location of a building that has been standing more than 50 years.
- The names of two people who make their living performing a service.
- The names of two people who make their living selling a product.
- Evidence of change.
- A problem facing our community.
- A natural resource.
- Something that makes our community a great place to live.

Treasure Hunt

Make a map of your community or part of the community where children could easily walk to. Write directions that will take them from the starting point to a "secret treasure." Write clues that include information about places in the area like, "walk three blocks down the oldest street in the community and turn left by the first church in community." Periodically you can have them make note of certain features or landmarks by saying something like "write the date on the corner stone on the building." Either arrange for students to pick up their treasure at the final destination or have parents verify that they have completed the treasure hunt and award the prizes in class.

Historic Drama

Perform a dramatic presentation of important historic events in your community's history.

Group Lessons

Places to Visit

Plan to make your unit on your community an action-oriented unit of study. Get out of the classroom and into the community. Take as many walking field trips as possible. Visit museums, historic areas, cultural centers, businesses and stores, governmental offices, transportation centers, communication centers, energy plants, building sites, cemeteries, churches, shopping centers, hospitals, geographical or geological locations, scientific centers, and zoos. Get out there and discover first-hand what is special about your community. In all cases, field trips should be well-planned so the results are educational. Before the trip, discuss what they might see and what questions they might like to ask. After the trip, follow up with a discussion or activity that will help students bring their observations into focus and apply them to their knowledge.

Special Speakers

When you can't get out of the classroom, bring speakers into the classroom. Send a letter to inform parents and community members of your unit of study and ask them for their support and contributions of time and information. Consider inviting the following people into your classroom to speak:

- museum curators
- members of the local historical society
- employees of the planning department
- representatives from the department of parks and recreation
- someone from the office of the mayor
- representatives from newspapers, television, and radio stations
- a real estate broker
- a representative from the chamber of commerce
- someone who has lived in the community a long time
- a local business owner
- someone who knows about the local geology, ecology or weather

Lesson 1 - Webbing

Begin the study of your community by making a webbing of all the things that make up a community. Start with the words "our community" in a central circle. As students supply ideas, add these on lines that radiate from the center. Add related ideas on branches of the lines. Be sure to include the major topics that are covered in this unit of study, either as indicated in this book or specific goals and information that you would like to cover with your class. Keep this webbing throughout your unit so you can refer back to it for ideas or add to it.

Lesson 2 - Assessing Knowledge

Ask students what they already know about their community. Make a list of concepts and specific information they discuss. Then ask them what they would like to find out about their community. Keep this list of questions in a prominent place throughout the unit so you can discuss answers to the questions as they are presented through guest lecturers, discussions, field trips, and study.

Lesson 3 - Personal Histories

Find out about the members of the class by asking students to stand up if:

- you were born here.
- you've lived here over three years.
- you moved here from some other place in the state.
- you are related to someone who lived here 100 years ago.
- you've been to the museum.
- you know an interesting fact about our community.
- you have ridden in some form of transportation besides a car or taxi.
- you know what special celebrations our community participates in.

Lesson 4 - **Location**

Ask students to imagine that they had to tell someone from another country how to find their community. How would they do it? Write ideas on the board as they are suggested. References should include the country, state, highways and roads, geographical features, and other towns.

Using an overhead projector or large map of your surrounding area, have individual students point out other towns, roads, and geographical features. Then give students directions, like "go from town A to town B," and have them trace the route on the map. Ask other students to judge whether the answers are correct by showing thumbs up for a correct response and thumbs down for an incorrect response.

Lesson 5 - **People**

Explain that communities are made of many different elements including buildings, streets, businesses, government, schools, churches, etc. The most important element, though, is people. Ask students to suggest why people are so important to a community. Bring out the idea that a community is made of people who help each other and depend on each other.

Tell students that you are going to tell them a story but you need their help. As you tell them a story about a little boy who lives in your community, you will mention places he goes to or situations he finds himself in, they are to suggest how another person helps him. For example, when you say that he goes to the store, students may suggest that a clerk helps him select and pay for a birthday present for a friend. When you say that he goes to the dentist, students may suggest that the dental hygenist cleans his teeth and shows him how to brush correctly. In each instance, his experience should involve some kind of a positive or helpful encounter with another person.

Lesson 6 - **Group Living**

Ask students to close their eyes and picture themselves living on a desert island all by themselves. Then discuss the fact that there are advantages to living in a community. Living in a community lets people do things as a group that would be more difficult or more expensive to do by themselves. As a group, make a list of advantages of living in a community. Break into groups of two or three and have each group choose one of the items from the list and pantomine it. Or have individual students complete the sentence "One advantage of living in a community is __" and draw a picture illustrating their sentence.

Lesson 7 - **Meeting Needs**

As a group, brainstorm a list of things you need to survive and live comfortably. Then discuss how these needs are met in your community. After the discussion, ask each student to pick a need and draw a picture of how the need is met by the community and write three sentences telling what the need is and how it is met. Display all the pictures together with the caption "Our needs are being met."

Lesson 8 - **Old Town**

Find out where "old town" is. Locate it on a map. Take a walking field trip through the old part of the community. Find things that tell you about the community long ago (cornerstones on buildings, dates in sidewalks, historic buildings, historic markers or monuments). Does the oldest part have a street called *Main, Central, First*, or *A*? Is it located near something that would have attracted early settlers or would have been one of their first buildings (church, fort, shipping facilities, storage area for farm products)? If you can get pictures of how this part of the community used to look, bring them along and compare them to what is presently there. What does the old community look like now? Is it old and dirty? Is it a rebuilt tourist area? Make rubbings of historic markers and cornerstones.

Lesson 9 - **Recreation**

Ask students to think about some of the things they or their families do in their spare time. Either have individual students pantomime one of their spare time activities or list the activities on the board. Then ask students to put their thumbs up if the recreational activity:

- is something you have done before
- is something you would like to do
- is related to our location or a natural resource in the area
- is done with other people
- attracts tourists to our community

Discuss and make note of the recreational activities that are available to the residents in your community that are directly related to its location or natural resources. Ask students to choose one of these activities and make a picture of themselves or their families engaged in this activity.

Lesson 10 - **Laws and Rules**

Tape up pieces of paper that have rules and laws written on them. Read them together. Ask, "What are these? Why do we need them? What would it be like if we didn't have any rules at all?" Ask, "What rules and laws do we have in this room that make it easier for people to get along and learn?"

Discuss the fact that a government is a group of elected people who make and enforce rules. They employ people like police and judges to help them.

Then ask students to suggest some rules that they think would be good for their community. List them as suggested. Have students individually choose the five rules that they think are the most important.

Lesson 11 - **Employment**

As a group, brainstorm a long list of all the jobs people in your community do. Classify them according to **Produces a product**, **Sells a product**, **Provides a service**, **Works for government**, and **Other**.

Lesson 12 - **Land Use**

Cut out squares or building shapes. Label each one with things found in a community—houses, school, hospital, factory, stores, farm, church, restaurant, etc. Attach tape to the back of each shape. Draw lines on the board to represent roads. Begin placing shapes randomly on the board so homes are next to factories and airports, stores next to farms, hospital and schools some distance from homes.

Ask students if they see any problems with this arrangement. How could they arrange it better?

Discuss:

- Why do we group housing, retail areas, and industrial uses?
- What things do we want close to houses? (schools, fire stations, hospitals) Why?
- Would it work to have a housing area next to an industrial area with shopping far away from the housing? Why?
- What problems are caused by mixing land uses?

Take down the shapes and label four streets *Rural Road*, *Business Boulevard*, *Industry Avenue*, and *Living Lane*. Have students place the shapes on the street they think is most appropriate.

Lesson 13 - **Communication**

Ask students, "Suppose you had an important announcement you wanted to get out to other people in our room, our school, or our community. How would you do it?" Make a list of the various means of communication as they are suggested.

Discuss:

- Which way is the quickest?
- Which way reaches the most people?
- Which way would be best to use with people your age?
- Why do people in a community need to communicate?

Call out different means of communication and have students pantomime something connected with that form of communication. For instance, if you say newspapers, they could act out writing a story, running the presses, interviewing someone, taking pictures, delivering the papers, or even reading a newspaper.

Lesson 14 - **Transportation**

As a group, have students make a list of all the different forms of transportation that are available in your community. Then give situations that involve getting from one place to another and have students suggest what mode of transportation they would use. For instance, you could say, "Suppose you wanted to go to the drug store. How would you get there?" Students could suggest walking, riding a bike, taking a bus, or driving a car. Use situations that involve going great distances as well as short distances and involve taking along baggage or cargo.

In conclusion, ask students to name the two kinds of transportation they use the most and the three kinds they use the least or have never used.

Lesson 15 - **Mystery Location**

Each day give the class a mystery location. The location could be described by an address, the intersection of two streets, or in reference to some other building or landmark. The next day ask how many students discovered what building, business, etc. was at the mystery location. Once the mystery location has been revealed, discuss the significance of the location. Discuss what activities or businesses are located there. Could the community do without these things? If so, how would things be different? Follow up by finding the location on a map. Repeat several times as a way of acquainting students with streets, places, and landmarks in your community.

Learning Centers

Categorizing Photos

Before you begin your study of your community, take pictures of various things around town—buildings, historical sites, people, businesses, recreational sites, etc. Put the photos in a box with instructions to categorize them in some way. You could provide the ideas for groupings or have students devise their own groupings and explain what these categories are.

Card Game

Make a card game that will allow students the opportunity to share their knowledge of the community. One set of cards should have letters of the alphabet written on them. Do not make cards for letters that begin only a few words. The second set of cards should have general descriptions of things that are found in communities in general or in your community in particular. Duplicate descriptions, if necessary, so you have at least 20 cards. You should not have the same number of cards in both decks. Descriptive cards can be things like:

- last name of someone in your community
- a street name
- a building
- a body of water
- a business

Students play by drawing two cards, one from each deck. They must then name something from your community that fits the description on the one card and begins with the letter on the other card. If they name something, they get a point. If they cannot name something, they do not get a point. The cards are then put at the bottom of the pile.

Marking Maps

Get a large map of your community and post it on a bulletin board. Color or mark the school, important landmarks or geographical features.

Information Cards

Make several information cards about special people, places and things in your community. Put a picture on the top half of each card. Write an interesting fact on the bottom. Cut each card in half in a unique fashion, like puzzle pieces. Mix up the pieces and have students match the two pieces of each card.

What We Have

Make cards that name things one normally finds in a city. Include both concrete items and abstract items and things your community has and does not have. Some ideas might be:

clean air
a mayor
a hospital
farmer's market
an airport
a harbor
quality life
theater

Ask students to categorize them according to "things our community does have" and "things our community does not have."

Businesses

Collect business cards from several businesses in the community. Have students categorize cards according to the following:

- services, products, other
- places you've been, places you haven't been
- some other categorization that seems appropriate.

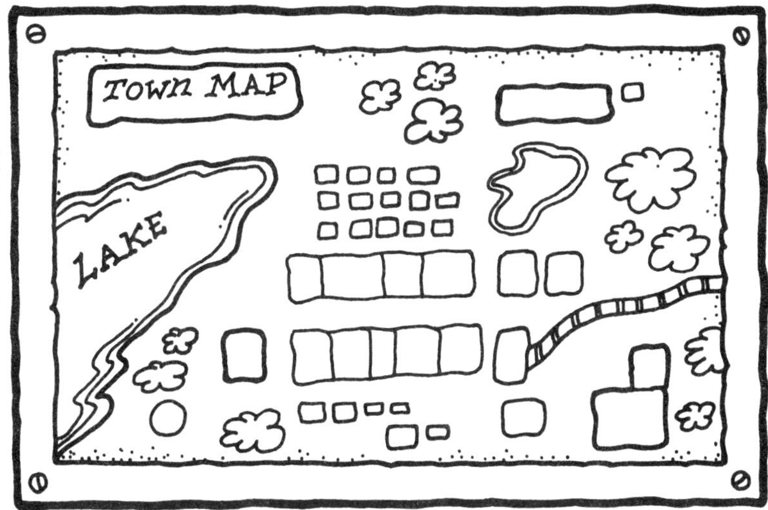

Our Community Circle

Name ____________________________

A community is made of many things. This circle shows some of the things that are part of a community. Cut out the pictures on the next page and paste them in the correct part of the circle.

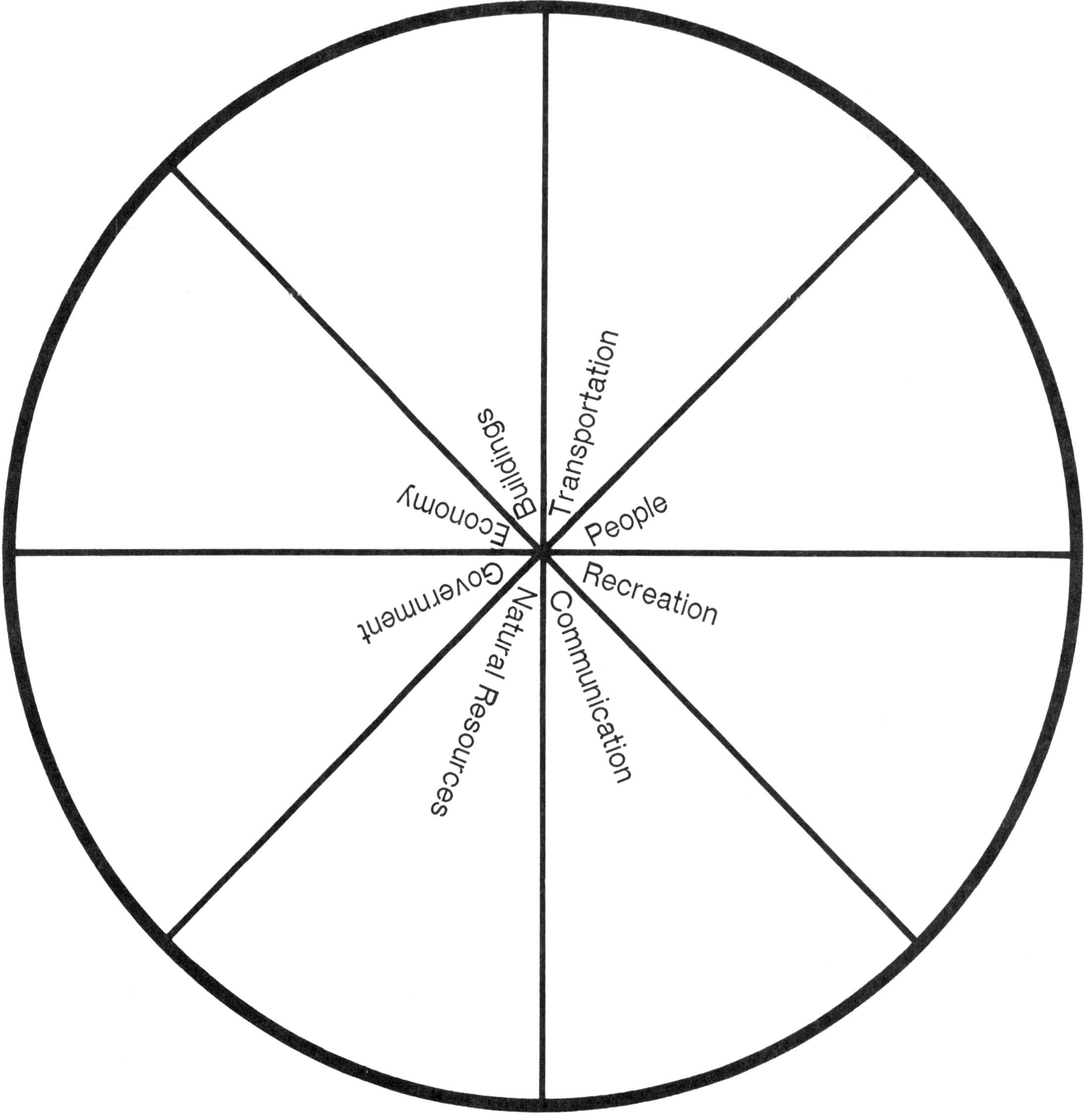

Our Community Circle

Name ______________________________

Cut out these pictures and paste them in the spaces on the community circle.

A Place in Space

Name ____________________

Answer these questions about the location of your community.

1. The name of our town is ____________________
2. It is located in the state of ____________________
3. Another town it is close to is ____________________
4. It is also close to ____________________
(a land form—ocean, lake, mountain, river, desert)
5. I have found our town on the following maps:
   - ☐ a map of our state
   - ☐ a map of our country
   - ☐ a globe or map of the world
6. To the north is ____________________

   To the south is ____________________

   To the west is ____________________

   To the east is ____________________
7. You can get to our town by
   - ☐ car, by following ____________________ (freeway, highway or main road)
   - ☐ bus
   - ☐ train
   - ☐ airplane
   - ☐ boat
   - ☐ other ____________________

Freeway
505

On Location

Name ______________________

People didn't build their towns just any place. They thought about what was good and bad about a place before they decided to settle there. Early settlers usually chose locations that had good farming, had minerals they could mine or trees they could cut, and had good transportation.

Check the things that your town has or is close to.

Transportation center
- ☐ railroad
- ☐ river
- ☐ sea port
- ☐ highway
- ☐ stagecoach stop
- ☐ ____________________

Natural resources
- ☐ minerals
- ☐ forest
- ☐ good farm or range land
- ☐ fishing
- ☐ ____________________

Recreation
- ☐ good weather
- ☐ water (lakes, rivers, ocean)
- ☐ mountains
- ☐ ____________________

Trade, learning or government center
- ☐ mission or fort
- ☐ manufacturing
- ☐ college or university
- ☐ state capital
- ☐ ____________________

Other
- ☐ good place for people to retire
- ☐ a place for people who work in a larger city to live
- ☐ ____________________
- ☐ ____________________

Something Extra

Things may be different today than they were when your town was settled. Find out why people first settled in your area. Then make a * by each thing above that was a reason for people to locate your town where it is.

Town Cryer

Name ______________________

Towns used to have town cryers. They were people who walked around the town and spread the news. Today towns have other ways to tell people the news. How do the people in your town find out what is happening?

Our town has a newspaper called the ______________________.

It is published _____ times a week.

We have ________ television stations.

One television station is called ________ on channel ________.

We also have ________ radio stations.

One radio station is called ________ on channel ________.

Put a **T** by the things you find on television, a **R** by the things you find on radio and a **N** for the things you find in newspapers. You may use more than one letter for each thing.

________ weather
________ news
________ information about sales in stores
________ cartoons
________ music
________ listings of homes for sale
________ advertisements
________ pictures
________ people's voices
________ sports information
________ comics
________ the correct time
________ food advertisements

Recreation

Name ______________________________

Communities often have places where people can relax, meet with each other, and learn about new things.

Check the things that your community has. Tell what you would do at each place.

☐ **zoo**

I would ______________________________

____

☐ **swimming pool or beach**

I would ______________________________

____

☐ **park**

I would ______________________________

____

☐ **gardens or greenhouses**

I would ______________________________

____

☐ **museum**

I would ______________________________

____

☐ **theater**

I would ______________________________

____

Name That Place

Name ______________________________

Communities have many different businesses. These businesses meet the needs of the people who live there. Write the name of a real business in your community for each type of business listed below. If your town does not have one of the businesses, leave it blank.

restaurant ______________________

drug store ______________________

shoe store ______________________

real estate office ______________________

motel ______________________

lumber yard ______________________

ice cream store ______________________

auto sales lot ______________________

jewelry store ______________________

medical center ______________________

theater ______________________

furniture store ______________________

photography shop ______________________

hardware store ______________________

hospital ______________________

auto repair shop ______________________

beauty salon ______________________

pet store ______________________

church ______________________

gas station ______________________

clothing store ______________________

florist ______________________

Something Extra
Choose one business and make a new sign for it.

Museums

Name ______________________________

Museums are places where collections of things are placed so people can come and learn about them. Many towns have historical museums that contain things from the past. There many other kinds of museums that contain everything from fossils to rocket ships.

Our community has _____ museums. They are:

- ☐ history
- ☐ science
- ☐ art
- ☐ natural history
- ☐ other __________________________

Visit one of the museums. Then tell what you saw, heard, or learned about at the museum by drawing a picture in this space.

Survey

Name ____________________________

People have different ideas about what is good or bad about their town. This is a chance for you to find out what other people think by taking a survey. This means that you will be asking many people the same question and recording their answers. You could ask a question like:

- Do we need more industry?
- Would you like to have a new shopping mall in town?
- Should we spend more money for a new park?
- Should every house be required to have a tree in its front yard?

1. Think of a question you would like to ask. It would be easiest if you asked a question that could be answered yes or no.
   My question is ____

2. Ask at least 10 to 20 people what they think about your question. Record their answers.

   Number who said yes ____________________________

   Number who said no ____________________________

3. Make a chart or graph on another piece of paper that shows how many people gave each answer.

4. Give the results of your survey to someone who could use this information.

Community Search

Name ______________________

Make a search of your community to find the following things.

1. Where can you find the cheapest gas? ______________________
2. Where can you find the biggest hamburger? ______________________
3. Who is one of the oldest residents? ______________________
4. What new development is happening? ______________________
5. What is the name of a service group (people who help other people)?

____

6. What are five plants that grow well in your area?

____

____

7. What is something people disagree about?

____

8. What animal naturally lives in your area? ______________________
9. What street corner is very busy? ______________________
10. Where can you find the best pizza? ______________________
11. Where can you find something that is changing? ______________________
12. Where can you find out how many people live in your community?

____

Standing on a Corner

Name ___________________________

You can learn a lot about your community and the people who live there just by standing on a corner and watching what is happening. You can watch the traffic and people go by. You can notice the kind of stores that are on corner locations. You may see problems (traffic jams, too many signs, people who are lost). You may also find that certain times of the day are busier than others.

Find a busy corner in your town. Stand there and watch what is happening. Tell what you saw or learned.

____

____

____

____

____

____

____

____

____

____

____

____

____

____

____

____

____

____

Vacant Lot Exploration

Name ____________________________

Spend some time exploring a vacant lot and use this sheet to tell about it.

I visited a vacant lot that is located ____________________________________

____

I saw ____

____

____

____

____

I heard ____

____

____

____

I thought about or learned ____

____

____

What I think we should do with this vacant lot is to _____________________

____

____

Rules

Name ___________________________

Communities have rules that help people live together peacefully. Usually the people who are elected to run your community decide what the rules are. The rules might be things like:

- You cannot dump your garbage in the river.
- You can only park your car in marked parking spaces.
- You cannot make loud noises that bother your neighbors.
- You cannot take things that don't belong to you.

Talk to some adults and find out what kind of rules your community has. What is one rule your town has that you think is a very good one?

____

____

If you could make up the rules for your town, what rules would you make?

____

____

____

____

____

____

Community Celebration

Name ______________________

Communities have celebrations. These sometimes celebrate something that happened a long time ago or honor the people who settled the community. Sometimes they celebrate national or religious holidays. They help people feel like they are a part of the community.

What celebration does your town have? ______________________

Why does it have this celebration? ______________________

____

What do people do during the celeration?

- ☐ have a parade
- ☐ have a picnic or barbeque
- ☐ dress in costumes
- ☐ have special contests
- ☐ have a carnival
- ☐ have special music
- ☐ have a rodeo
- ☐ have special shows or exhibits
- ☐ other ______________________

____

Something Extra

Think of a new celebration for your community. What will you celebrate? Think about what your celebration will be like. Make a list of everything people will do. Then draw a poster telling people about the celebration.

Personality Plus

Name ___________________________

Communities have personalities. Some are large. Some are small. Some are noisy, and others are quiet. Think about your community and its personality. Check the words that describe your town.

- ☐ old
- ☐ young
- ☐ middle-aged
- ☐ big
- ☐ middle-sized
- ☐ small
- ☐ noisy
- ☐ quiet
- ☐ easy-going
- ☐ full of energy
- ☐ pretty
- ☐ average-looking
- ☐ ugly
- ☐ unusual
- ☐ sparkling
- ☐ dull
- ☐ changing
- ☐ improving

What other words would you use to describe your community?

during the summer ___________________________

during the winter ___________________________

in the middle of the day ___________________________

late at night ___________________________

during a special holiday ___________________________

Our Community is Like . . .

Name ______________________

Fill in the blanks with words to describe your town.

Our community is sometimes as quiet as ______________________

Our community is sometimes as noisy as ______________________

Our community sometimes smells like ______________________

Our community is sometimes as lively as ______________________

Our community moves as fast as ______________________

Is your community more like a motorcycle or a bicycle? ______________

Why? ______________________

Is your community more like a freeway or a quiet road? ______________

Why? ______________________

Is your community more like a flower or a giant tree? ______________

Why? ______________________

Is your community more like a clear lake or a dirty pond? ______________

Why? ______________________

A Special Place

Name ______________________

Find a place in your community where you could do the following things. Tell where that place is.

Where you can feel free ______________________

Where you can run and jump ______________________

Where you can learn new things ______________________

Where you can be quiet ______________________

Where you can see beautiful colors ______________________

Where you can smell things that smell good ______________________

Where you can remember things that make you happy

____

Where you can help other people ______________________

Where your whole family can have a good time ______________________

Where you can see and touch nature ______________________

Where you can see a piece of history ______________________

Where you can go for a hike ______________________

Heart Throb

Name ____________________________

Talk to several people to find out what they think is special about your community. Then fill in this heart with pictures or words to tell what makes your town special.

The heart of our community is . . .

A, B, C's of Our Community

Name ______________________________

Write a word for each letter of the alphabet that describes your community or names something special that can be found in your town.

A ______________________________

B ______________________________

C ______________________________

D ______________________________

E ______________________________

F ______________________________

G ______________________________

H ______________________________

I ______________________________

J ______________________________

K ______________________________

L ______________________________

M ______________________________

N ______________________________

O ______________________________

P ______________________________

Q ______________________________

R ______________________________

S ______________________________

T ______________________________

U ______________________________

V ______________________________

W ______________________________

X ______________________________

Y ______________________________

Z ______________________________

How Does Your Community Rate?

Name ______________________________

Mark one box in each line to tell how you think your community rates in each area listed below. On the line tell why you feel this way.

Size ☐ too big ☐ just right ☐ too small

Why? ______________________________

Weather ☐ good ☐ okay ☐ not so good

Why? ______________________________

Schools ☐ good ☐ okay ☐ not so good

Why? ______________________________

Parks ☐ good ☐ okay ☐ not so good

Why? ______________________________

Activities for children ☐ good ☐ okay ☐ not so good

Why? ______________________________

Friendly, helpful people ☐ good ☐ okay ☐ not so good

Why? ______________________________

Housing ☐ good ☐ okay ☐ not so good

Why? ______________________________

Newspapers, radio, television ☐ good ☐ okay ☐ not so good

Why? ______________________________

A New Business

Name ______________________

All communities have stores and businesses that provide goods and services for the people who live there. People often start a new business because they see something that the people in the community need that is not being offered by other businesses.

Pretend that you could open a business in your community that people your age would love. Use the space below to describe your new business.

My business will be ______________________

It will provide the people with ______________________

I will call my business ______________________

Kids will love my business because ______________________

____

The sign for my business will look like this.

Buildings

Name ______________________

Usually buildings are designed to fit the weather and the land and to use building materials that are available. Look at the buildings in your community. Are they all different or are some things the same? Are the buildings built for a hot climate or a cold one? Are they built for flat land or steep hills?

Describe the buildings in your community.

____

____

____

____

Now that you have studied the buildings in your community, you can design your own building. Think about what kind of building is needed in your town.

Describe what your building will be used for.

____

Where will the building be located?

____

On the back of this paper or on another piece of paper draw your building.

Learning About Jobs

Name ______________________

Communities are made of people who have jobs (either within their own home or outside their home) that help the community and the other people. Find out what one person in your community does by talking to him or her. Make a list of questions to ask this person.

I talked to ______________________ who

- ☐ makes a product
- ☐ helps other people
- ☐ sells ______________________
- ☐ other ______________________

These are the questions I asked.

____

____

____

This is what I learned

____

____

____

____

____

____

____

____

____

Land Use

Name ______________________________

People own the land in communities. Some people just want to build a house on their land. Other people what to build businesses, apartments, factories, and other things on their land. Some of these ways of using land go well together (are compatible) and some do not.

Look at the following groups of things. Think about what it would be like if these things were next to each other. If they go together, circle **yes**. If they do not go together, circle **no**.

yes	no	**pig farm**	**office building**
yes	no	**school**	**houses**
yes	no	**fire station**	**police station**
yes	no	**hospital**	**noisy factory**
yes	no	**gift store**	**bakery**
yes	no	**dairy farm**	**cheese making plant**
yes	no	**hotel**	**restaurant**
yes	no	**junk yard**	**jewelry store**

What two things can you think of that would be good if they were next to each other in your town?

____

What two things would not be good next to each other?

____

Good Citizens

Name ______________________

A community needs lots of good citizens. These are people who do their part to make their community a good place to live for all people. Check the things below that describe a good citizen.

- ☐ obeys laws
- ☐ throws garbage on the ground
- ☐ thinks about other people
- ☐ is selfish
- ☐ helps other people
- ☐ is kind
- ☐ is rude and pushy
- ☐ works to make the town a better place to live
- ☐ respects other people's rights
- ☐ makes a lot of noise

In your own words, tell what it means to be a good citizen.

____

____

Something Extra

Make a good citizen award. Give it to someone in your community who deserves it.

Signs

Name ______________________

There are many uses for signs. They can tell people where to go, tell them what to do and what not to do, or inform them of points of interest. Look at the signs around your town. Then make new signs to help your town in some way.

1.

2.

3.

4.

Tell where you would put each sign.

1. ______________________ 3. ______________________

2. ______________________ 4. ______________________

Landmark

Name ______________________

Many communities have landmarks or monuments to point out places where something important happened long ago. They mark places that people usually find interesting. Think about your community, its history, and its most interesting places. Then design a landmark or monument for your community. Draw it in the space below.

Where would this monument or landmark be located?

____

Community Flag

Name ______________________________

Many communities have flags they fly outside their government offices and on special days. A flag usually shows something that is special about the community (its history, its location, or a natural resource). It may have a motto, a special saying that tells something about the community. It also will have the name of the community and sometimes the date it was founded.

Design a flag for your community that tells what is special about it.

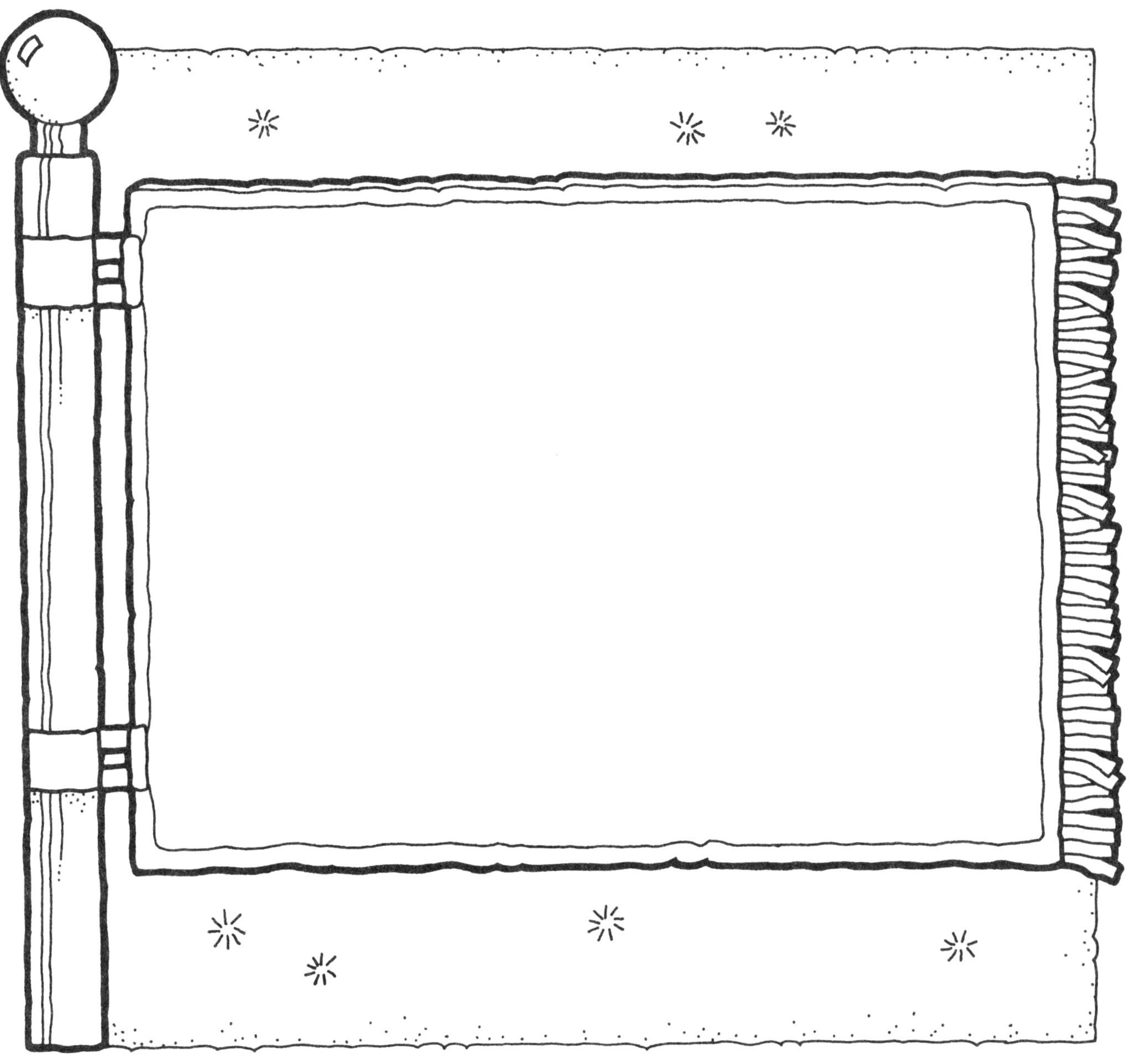

Have I Got a Problem

Name ___________________________

It would be hard if you had to live by yourself. You would have to do everything for yourself, without the help of other people. By living in a community, though, you have many people and businesses that can help you solve problems and get what you need.

Get out the business section of your local telephone directory and tell who you would call or where you would go for each of these things. Write the name and phone number.

1. Your sink is plugged ___________________________
2. You need new tennis shoes ___________________________
3. You need someone to take care of your dog while you are on vacation ___________________________
4. You broke your leg ___________________________
5. You need a new tire for your bike ___________________________
6. You want to sell your old bike ___________________________
7. You need a haircut ___________________________
8. You need the materials to build a treehouse ___________________________
9. You want to buy your brother a baseball for his birthday ___________________________
10. You want to open a savings account with the money you got for your birthday ___________________________

SHOE STORE

DOCTORS

BUILDING SUPPLIES

DIRECTORY

Changes for the Better

Name ____________________________

Communities are always changing. Old things are torn down and new things are built in their places. Communities change to become more modern, to work better, to meet the needs of the people who live there, and to solve problems. Think about the changes you would like to make in your community. Then complete the sentences below.

If you were in charge of change in your community, what would you like to:

Keep just the way it is? ____________________________

Make bigger? ____________________________

Move to another location? ____________________________

Remodel? ____________________________

Tear down? ____________________________

Keep the way it was 50 years ago? ____________________________

Have more of? ____________________________

Make more colorful? ____________________________

Divide into pieces or spaces? ____________________________

Make smaller? ____________________________

Government

Name ____________________________

Almost all communities have governments. The government provides things that would be very hard or very expensive for each family to get on its own. The government collects tax money from all the people. Then it uses the money to buy things like parks or provide services like police protection for all the people.

Some of the words in the list below are things that are provided by governments. Choose six things that are provided by the goverment in your community. Write the words in the bubbles.

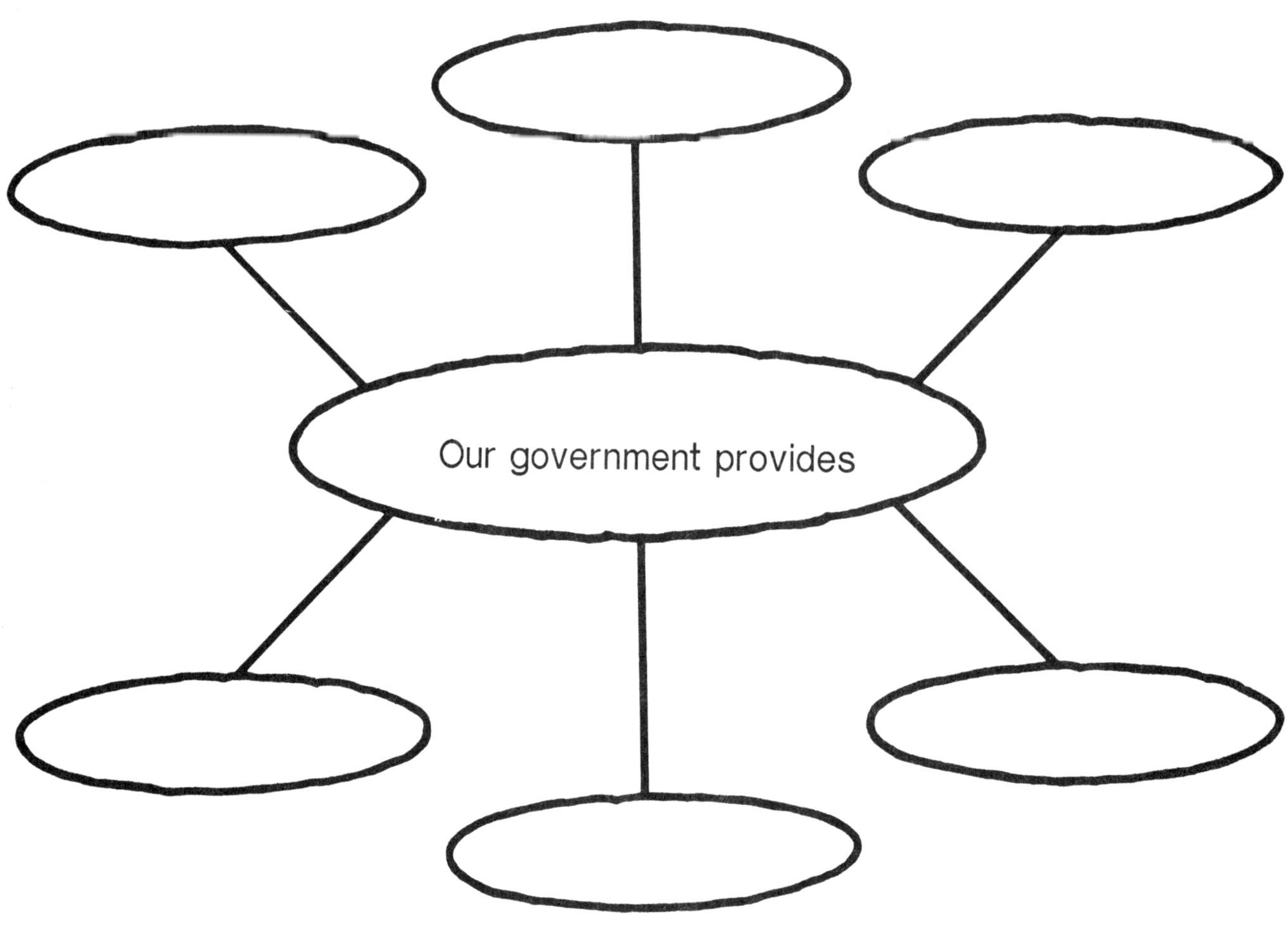

police protection
shoes
schools
parks

cars
water
movies
libraries

restaurants
sewers
fire protection
roads

Dateline--Our Town

Write a newspaper article about something that is happening in your community. First write a short answer to the five questions. Then write your article.

Who ______________________________

What ______________________________

Where ______________________________

When ______________________________

Why ______________________________

Our Town Gazette

headline ______________________________

date______________ Reporter______________

Historic People

Name ____________________________

Choose someone who played an important part in the history of your community. Find out everything you can about his person. Then use this space to make a tombstone for him or her. Include the following things:

- the name of the person
- date of birth and date of death
- a saying that tells something about him or her
- a drawing or design

If you could meet this person, what is one question you would like to ask?

____

Kids' Economy

Name ____________________

People used to just trade things they needed. Now people use money to buy things they need and to pay for services. Pretend you have $100. What goods and services in your community would you spend your money on? Make a list below of how you would spend your money. You cannot spend more that $15 at any one kind of business.

Amount	Business Name	For

$100.00 = Total

Getting There

Name ______________________

Make a check by the kind of transportation that is available in your community.

___ car
___ taxi
___ subway
___ monorail
___ bus
___ railroad
___ boat
___ walking
___ bicycle
___ airplane
___ other ______________________

Think about how people in the future will get from one place to another in your community. Describe your new form of transportation and draw a picture of it on another piece of paper.

____

____

____

____

____

Our Town or Bust

Name ______________________________

Why did people first come to your community? Find out why the first settlers chose the location they did. Then pretend you are an early settler. Write a letter to your cousin telling about why you have chosen to live in your community. Try to convince your cousin to move to this same community.

Date ____________________

Dear Cousin,

Here we are in ______________________________ . We have decided to settle here because ____

____

____

____

____

____

____

____

____

____

Sincerely,

Jobs

Name ________________________

When people live together in groups (like communities) there is a **division of labor**. This means that each person has a different job. They do not do everything themselves. People buy goods and services from each other. People in a community have many different kinds of jobs.

Make a check in the box that best describes what each of these people do.

Makes a product	Sells a product	Provides a service	
☐	☐	☐	librarian
☐	☐	☐	car repair person
☐	☐	☐	nurse
☐	☐	☐	artist
☐	☐	☐	cabinet maker
☐	☐	☐	auto factory worker
☐	☐	☐	grocery store owner
☐	☐	☐	mayor
☐	☐	☐	police officer
☐	☐	☐	farmer
☐	☐	☐	gardener
☐	☐	☐	zoo keeper
☐	☐	☐	weather forecaster
☐	☐	☐	teacher
☐	☐	☐	baker
☐	☐	☐	candy store owner
☐	☐	☐	builder
☐	☐	☐	dry cleaner
☐	☐	☐	photographer
☐	☐	☐	taxi driver
☐	☐	☐	ice cream store owner

Liking Your Location

Name ______________________

Think about where your community is located. What are all the good things about this location? Here is a list of things that are good about locations. Cross out the ones that do **not** apply to your location. At the bottom, add your own ideas about what is good about your location.

good weather
pretty scenery
fertile farm land
close to water
close to mountains
clean
lots of recreation
easy to get to (transportation center)
good harbor for shipping
lots of natural resources
quiet and peaceful

____

____

____

Tell what is **not** good about where your community is located.

____

____

____

Going and Growing

Name ____________________

Most communities have more people living in them today than they did in the past. Your teacher will give you the numbers you need to fill in this chart.

Time	Population
100 years ago	______________
50 years ago	______________
25 years ago	______________
now	______________

1890 POPULATION
1940 POPULATION
1965 POPULATION
1890 .... 2567 pop.
1940 .... 15,000 pop.
1965 .... 42,507 pop.

Use these numbers to make a graph showing how the population of your community has grown.

-100 years	-50 years	-25 years	now

time

Tell what you think the population will be in 25 years. ______________

1. Picture Display

Get a camera and take pictures of several of the buildings in your community. Group them in some way (by size, use, or some other way). Make a display of your pictures in their groupings.

2. Comparing Communities

Compare your community with another community that you have visited. Make a chart that shows how they compare in size, population, location, weather, and any other ways you have found that they are alike or different.

3. A Beautiful Plan

How would you make your community more beautiful? Make a plan that tells everything you would do.

4. Shopping Center Map

If your community has a shopping center, make a map of the center. Then draw a trail that goes to your favorite places in the shopping center. Tell all the good and not-so-good things about having a shopping center in your community.

5. Community Facts

Pretend you are a tour guide. Make a list of interesting facts about the places and buildings in your community. Put them on cards or on a tape recording. Make a map to show where these places are located.

6. Street Names

Look at the names of the streets in your community. Group some of the streets on a chart with these headings:

foreign words	**peoples' names**
trees	**numbers**
descriptions	**other**

7. Historic Rubbing

Make a rubbing of a plaque on a building, a tombstone in a cemetery, or a landmark that shows something about your community's history. Write a short description of the building, tombstone, or landmark and explain what it tells about your community's history.

8. Historic Comparison

How is your community different today than it was 100 years ago? Make a chart labeled **Now** and **Then** that shows the differences.

9. Letter to the Future

Make a tape recording or write a letter to a child in the future telling him or her what it is like to live in your community now and what changes you would like to see in the future.

10. Masquerade

Dress up as someone who lived in your community long ago. Tell a story about what it was like to live then.

11. City Symbols

Does your community have a motto, symbol, button, historical marker, or sign? If not, make one that will reflect something special about your community.

12. Our Town Game

Make a monopoly game board using places and streets from your community.

13. Something Special

Make a large poster that shows something about your community. You can show something from its past, a place, a feature like a mountain or river, something that can be seen in your town that you cannot see anywhere else, or anything else that is special about your community. Hang the poster where other people can see it.

14. Map Marking

Get a map of your community and mark and label one of the following:

- points of interest
- a walk other people would enjoy
- historical sites
- the most attractive buildings
- places that produce pollution

15. Our Town Collage

Make a collage that tells about your community. Cut out or draw pictures and words. Arrange them on a large piece of paper. When it looks just the way you want, paste all the items in place.

16. A Campaign for Change

What does your community need now? Start a campaign to make a change in your community (get people to pick up garbage, put in street lights, paint crosswalks, plant trees, or anything you think your community really needs). Convince other people to help you.

17. Mobile

Make a mobile that tells about your community. Cut out pictures and write words and glue them to both sides of four pieces of paper. On another piece of paper, write the name of your community. Get two sticks and some string. Hang the pieces on the sticks to make a mobile.

18. Opinion Banner

Make a banner that shows how you feel about your community. Draw pictures or use words to show your feelings. On one side show the things you like. On the other side, show the things you don't like.